D1524918

Shakespeare
on Baseball

Shakespeare on Baseball

"Such Time–Beguiling Sport"

Compiled by David Goodnough

BARRICADE
BOOKS

New York•New York

Published by Barricade Books Inc.
150 Fifth Avenue
Suite 700
New York, NY 10011
Visit our website at:
www.barricadebooks.com

Copyright © 2000 by David Goodnough
Illustrations by Bob Schochet
All Rights Reserved.

Library of Congress Cataloging-in-Publication Data
Shakespeare, William, 1564-1616.
    Shakespeare on baseball : such time-beguiling
sport / compiled by David Goodnough.
        p. cm.
    ISBN 1-56980-139-8 (alk. paper)
    1. Shakespeare, William, 1564-1616--
Quotations. 2. Baseball Quotations, maxims, etc. I.
Goodnough, David. II. Title.
PR2892.G66 2000
822.3'3--dc21   99-32371
                                                      CIP
Printed in the United States of America.
10 9 8 7 6 5 4 3 2 1

Pre-Game Show

Wﬁlliam Shakespeare was the greatest
baseball writer the game has ever
known. This is a statement so true
that—as H. Allen Smith said of his claim to be
the world's greatest authority on chili—it should
be entered in all the major encyclopedias and
inscribed on the front of public buildings. Of
course, this has been said of other sportswriters—
Grantland Rice, Red Smith, Arthur Daley come to
mind—but have you ever noticed that when their
invention flagged, when they were searching for
the precise word or phrase, the exact shade of
meaning, how often they turned to the works of
Sweet Will, as he was nicknamed (see Sonnet
CXXXVI)? Sometimes they didn't even credit
their source and introduced his immortal words
into their copy without so much as a thank you.
Ah, but Sweet Will was no stranger to ingratitude
(see his *King Lear*—he wrote plays during the
off–season) and injustice (see *The Merchant of
Venice*, and a whole slew of others), not to mention
outright jealousy (see *Othello*, in which, by the
way, Sweet Will was the first to break the color
barrier—*pace* Branch Rickey).

That having been said, we might ask our-
selves, who was this kid who came out of the

5

minors and stood London on its ear? I don't think there is any doubt that he was once a player— there is just too much internal evidence in his work to believe otherwise—but we have no idea what position he played or for how long. The game was called rounders in those days, and they hadn't gotten around to keeping records, although Sweet Will does refer to what seem to be stats (*q.v.*). I suspect his actual playing career was short, perhaps because of a weight problem to which he alludes often, albeit when speaking generally or of others. No, I believe he made his mark, while active, as a coach or manager. That he knew the game inside and out is beyond question, but there is another dimension to him that indicates a deeper understanding of the game and of those who play it than one usually finds in your average player. I can think of one instance—in *Hamlet* I believe—where he gives his players a whole list of things they should or should not do if they appear on, say, the Renaissance equivalent of post–game interviews, talk shows, or Hall of Fame inductions. I don't think it would be stretching things to say that if modern players took heed of such advice it would spare all of us a great deal of needless embarrassment.

Anyway, whether he was player, coach, or manager boots little, for it was as a writer that he achieved his niche in the pantheon of baseball's immortals. One of the amazing things about his work, though, was its pre–cognition. It is as though he had the ability to read the future and divine things that are happening today as if they happened long ago, if you get my drift. Like his precursor Nostradamus (who, I know for a fact, came up with the Mets' 1986 win in the World Series though writing more than 400 years ago), his words need some interpretation, but the truth is there if you can ken it.

But when it comes right down to it, Sweet Will's main contribution to the game is that he described it, as he said more than once, "right on." None of this hysterical "The Giants win the pennant! The Giants win the pennant! The Giants win the pennant!" nonsense. (Although it must be admitted he did go overboard at times: See him on grand slams.) So whenever you hear some announcer butchering our precious mother tongue, or read some reporter laboring over an improbable metaphor, or listen to a commentator's limp and lame alliterations, turn to these following pages for the real nitty. As a lagniappe, perhaps you will find here surcease from sorrow, joy in the morning and reflection in the evening, and, yes, some insight into the mysteries of the human heart. So here's to Sweet Will. Taken all in all, we shall not see his like again. Except I kind of like the looks of this young kid Mike Lupica out of New York.

Play Ball!

Abner Doubleday

Who did guide,
I mean, who set the body and the limbs
Of this great sport together, as you guess?

–King Henry VIII, I.i

Acting Commissioner

To say nothing, to do nothing, to know nothing, and to
have nothing, is to be a great part of your title; which is
within a very little of nothing.

–All's Well that Ends Well, II.iv

After batting around in the top of the ninth inning

Our revels now are ended.

–The Tempest, IV.i

All–Star Game

Why this is very midsummer madness.

–Twelfth Night, III.iv

Ambitious pitcher facing league's leading hitter

Thy turn is next, and then the rest;
Counting myself but bad till I be best.
—*King Henry VI, Part III, V.vi*

American League fan's opinion of the other league

O inglorious league!
—*King John, V.i*

American League pitcher's first at bat in National League

Poor harmless fly.
—*Titus Andronicus, III.ii*

Artificial turf

Why, these balls bound; there's noise in it.—
'Tis hard.
—*All's Well That Ends Well, II.iii*

Babe Ruth

Why, man, he doth bestride the narrow earth
Like a Colossus.
—*Julius Ceasar, I.ii*

A MID SUMMER NIGHT'S DREAM

12

Back–to–back Texas League singles

Why, is not this a lamentable thing, that we
should
be thus afflicted with these strange flies?
—Romeo and Juliet, II.iv

Bad press coverage

Why should calamity be full of words?
—King Richard III, IV.iv

Ballplayers

The wealthy curled darlings of our nation.
—Othello, I.i

Baseball as metaphor for life

Thus sometimes hath the brightest day a cloud;
And after summer evermore succeeds
Barren winter, with his wrathful nipping cold:
So cares and joys abound, as seasons fleet.
—King Henry VI, Part II, II,iv

Baserunner given the green light

By heaven, I'll steal away.
—All's Well That Ends Well, II.i

Batter facing knuckleballer with count at 3 and 0

My lord, I'll hit him now.

—Hamlet, V.ii

Batter facing Roger Clemens with count at 3 and 2

Something wicked this way comes.

—Macbeth, IV.i

Batter questioning line umpire's strike call

And will you credit this base drudge's words,
That speaks he knows not what?

—King Henry VI, Part II, IV.ii

Batting crown winner to last year's winner

You won it, wore it, kept it, gave it me.

—King Henry IV, Part II, IV.v

Beer endorsement

Make my image but an alehouse sign.

—King Henry VI, Part II, III.ii

Bench–clearing brawl

Are you not ashamed
With this immodest clamorous outrage?

–King Henry VI, Part I, IV.i

Bench coach

O, understand my drift.

–The Merry Wives of Windsor, II.ii

Bench jockeys

They will spit.

–As You Like It, IV.i

Bill Buckner after sixth game of 1986 Series

Had I but died an hour before this chance,
I had liv'd a blessed time, for from this instant,
There's nothing serious in mortality.
All is but toys, renown and grace is dead.
The wine of life is drawn, and the mere lees
Is left this vault to brag of.

–Macbeth, II.iii

Blame for missed double play

On him I lay that you would lay on me.

–King Richard III, III.vii

Bob Uecker

I am not only witty in myself, but the cause
that wit is in other men.

–King Henry IV, Part I, ii

Bottom of the ninth loss

Let us seek out some desolate shade, and there
Weep our sad bosoms empty.

–Macbeth, IV.iii

Boston: The day the Red Sox traded Roger Clemens

O woe! O woeful, woeful, woeful day!
Most lamentable day, most woeful day,
That ever, ever, I did yet behold!
O day! O day! O day! O hateful day!
Never was seen so black a day as this:
O woeful day, O woeful day!

–Romeo and Juliet, IV.v

Boston Globe's 1986 Series summary

If you have tears, prepare to shed them now
–Julius Caesar, III.ii.

Box scores

This news is old enough, yet it is every day's
news.

–Measure for Measure, III.ii

Bragging infielder

Then there's my glove.

–Timon of Athens, V.iv

Brushback sign from the bench

Knock him down there.

–King Henry VI, Part II, IV.vi

Bucky Dent's homer in the division playoff of the 1978 season

What a blow was there given!

–The Tempest, II.ii

Butterfingered infielder

And when he caught it, he let it go again; and
after it again; and over and over he comes, and
up again; catcht it again; or
whether his fall enraged him, or how 'twas, he
did so set his teeth, and tear it.

–Coriolanus, I.iii

Cal Ripken, Jr.

He has his health, and ampler strength indeed
Than most men have of his age.

–The Winter's Tale, IV.iv

Call for team meeting

For I have neither wit, nor words, nor worth,
Action, nor utterance, nor the power of speech,
To stir men's blood: I only speak right on;
I tell you that which you yourselves do know.

–Julius Caesar, III.ii

Candlestick Park on a mild day

Blow, winds, and crack your cheeks! rage! blow!
You cataracts and hurricanoes, spout!

–King Lear, III.ii

Casey Stengel

If you look for a good speech now, you undo me:
for what I have to say is of my own making; and
what indeed I should say will, I doubt, prove
mine own marring.

–King Henry IV, Part II, Epilogue

Casey Stengle, Yogi Berra, Billy Martin, et al.

Witness the entertainment that he gave.
—Venus and Adonis, l. 1108

Catcher minus his equipment

Thou art the thing itself; unaccommodated man.
—King Lear, III.iv

Caught stealing by a mile

And rather proved the sliding of your brother
A merriment than a vice.
—Measure for Measure, II.iv

Cecil Fielder, David Wells, et al.

He's fat, and scant of breath.
—Hamlet, V.ii

Clearing the bench

We must have bloody noses and crackt crowns,
And pass them current too.
—King Henry IV, Part I, II.iii

Close–mouthed pitching coach

For, you know,
Pitchers have ears.
–The Taming of the Shrew, IV, iv

Close play at home

That's monstrous: O, that that were out!
–The Two Gentlemen of Verona, III.i

Close stretch drive

All is uneven
And everything is left at six and seven.
–King Richard II, II.ii

Closing pitcher traded after retiring one batter

He is gone to save far off,
Whilst others come to make him lose at home.
–King Richrd II, II.ii

Club Owners

Their love
Lies in their purses.
–King Richard II, II.ii

Clubhouse blues

And do not drop in for an after–loss:
Ah! do not, when my heart hath scap'd this
    sorrow,
Come in the rearward of a conquer'd woe;
Give not a windy night a rainy morrow.
To linger out a purpos'd overthrow.

                –Sonnet XC

Clubhouse prayer group

Heaven prosper our sport!

    –The Merry Wives of Windsor, V.ii

Cocky pitcher facing .350 hitter

Will make him fly an ordinary pitch
Who else would soar above the view of men
And keep us all in servile fearfulness.

           –Julius Ceasar, I.i

Come–from–behind win in extra innings

So foul and fair a day I have not seen.

           –Macbeth, I.iii

Coming up in the bottom of the ninth in a tie game

This blow
Might be the be–all and end–all here.

–Macbeth, I.vii

Coming up with bases loaded and two outs

The rest will ne'er come in, if he be out.

–Love's Labour's Lost, V,ii

Commissioner A. Bartlett Giamatti on Pete Rose

And I will call him to so strict account
That he shall render every glory up.

–King Henry IV, Part I, III.ii

Condescending interviewer

Why does he suffer this rude knave now to
    knock him?

–Hamlet, V.i

Confident outfielder

And so I shall catch the fly.

–King Henry V, V.ii

Confident relief pitcher facing top of the order

I will strike it out soundly.

—King Henry V, IV.vii

Confident starter

And he that hits me, let him be clapt on the shoulder,
and called Adam.

—Much Ado About Nothing, I.i

Confused Manager

Now let us understand. There is three umpires in this
matter, as I understand.

—The Merry Wives of Windsor, I.i

Continuing slump

Hath all his ventures fail'd? What, not one hit?

—The Merchant of Venice, III.ii

Critical sportswriters

Poor breathing orators of miseries,!
Let them have scope.

—King Richard III, IV.iv

Crossed–up catcher

But thou didst understand me by my signs.
–King John, IV.ii

Crowd reaction to close call by umpire

When he hath ceas'd his ill–sounding noise,
Another flap–mouthed mourner, black and
    grim,
Against the welkin vollies out his voice;
Another and another answer him,
Clapping their proud tails to the ground below.
–Venus and Adonis, ll. 919–23

Crude dugout behavior

I shall break my wind.
–King Henry IV, Part I, II.ii

David Wells

Who's his tailor?
–All's Well That Ends Well, II.v

Desperate for baserunners

O, let me see thee walk.
–The Taming of the Shrew, II.i

Disgruntled manager to ump after being tossed

Here is my journey's end and here is my butt.

–Othello, V.ii

Dislocation or separation

O, good sir, softly, good sir! I fear, sir, my shoulder–blade is out.

–The Winter's Tale, IV.iii

Division clincher

O most courageous day! O most happy hour!

–A Midsummer Night's Dream, IV.ii

Domed stadium

Look you, this brave o'erhanging firmament, this majestical
roof fretted with golden fire, why, it appears no other thing
to me but a foul and pestilent congregation of vapours.

–Hamlet, II.ii

Don Drysdale, Bob Gibson, et al.

Who sets me else? by heaven, I'll throw at all.

–King Richard II, IV.i

Don Mattingly

As many farewells as be stars in heaven.

–Troilus and Cressida, IV.iv

Double header

A summer's day will seem an hour but short,
Being wasted in such time–beguiling sport.

–Venus and Adonis, ll. 23–24

Double–play ball, from pitcher's perspective

Thou hast most kindly hit it.

–Romeo and Juliet, II.iv

Double–play ball from batter's perspective

God damn me.

–The Comedy of Errors, IV.iii

Double steal – I

Stand not upon the order of your going,
But go at once.

–Macbeth, III.iv

Double steal – II
Pull't off, I say.

–Macbeth, V.iii

Double steal with two out and pitcher at plate
Though this be madness, yet there is method in't.

–Hamlet, II.ii

Dugout etiquette
Shall we clap into't roundly, without hawking or spitting?

–As You Like It, V.iii

Earl Weaver
You are most hot and furious when you win.

–Cymbaline, II.iii

Eddie Murray
I love not many words.

–All's Well That Ends Well, III.vi

End of the American League DH Rule

'Tis a consummation
Devoutly to be wisht.

−Hamlet, III.i

Entertaining visiting royalty

This way, my lord, for this way lies the game.

−King Henry VI, Part III, IV.v

Envious hitter

He does it with a better grace, but I do it more
    natural.

−Twelfth Night, II.iii

Envious manager on rival's pitching rotation

I would my arms could match thee in contention.

−Troulus and Cressida, IV.v

Envious pitching coach on rival's bullpen

Thou hast lusty arms.

−Troilus and Cressida, IV.v

THUS FAR OUR FORTUNE KEEPS AN UPWARD COURSE,
AND WE ARE GRACED WITH WREATHS OF VICTORY.
KING HENRY VI, PART III, V.iii

EARLY · SEASON WINNING STREAK

Error by cut–off man

Like to a bowl upon a subtle ground,
I have tumbled past the throw.

–Coriolanus, V.ii

Expansion teams

Betwixt mine eye and heart a league is took,
And each doth good turns now unto the other.

–Sonnet XLVII

Expansion team's prospects for a title

If it be now, 'tis not to come; if it be not to come,
it will be now; if it be not now, yet it will come:
the readiness is all.

–Hamlet, V.ii

Extra early morning batting practice

To business that we love we rise betime,
And go to't with delight.

–Antony and Cleopatra, IV.iv

Extra–innings loss

The expense of spirit in a waste of shame.

–Sonnet CXXIX

Failure to run out easy ground ball

Play out the play.

—King Henry IV, Part I, II.iv

Faking squeeze and then hitting away

If this should fail,
And that our drift look through our bad
    performance,
'Twere better not assay'd.

—Hamlet, IV.vii

Fan reaction to first woman TV announcer

Shut your mouth, dame.

—King Lear, V.iii

Fans leaving early

Now spurs the lated traveller apace
To gain the timely inn.

—Macbeth, III.iii

Fast ball, cutter, splitter, slider, sinker, curve, and changeup

We are such stuff
As dreams are made on.

–The Tempest, IV.i

Fast ball belt high and straight down the middle

As You Like It

Fastidious winning manager doused with champagne

I could well wish courtesy would invent some other custom of entertainment.

–Othello, II.iii

Fed–up fan

Of folded schedules had she many a one,
Which she perus'd, sigh'd, tore, and gave the
flood.

–A Lover's Complaint, ll. 44–45

Fibbing pitcher

Confess, confess, hath he not hit you here?

–The Taming of the Shrew, V.ii

Fielder who's lost his cool

That one error
Fills him with faults; makes him run through all
th' sins.

—The Two Gentlemen of Verona, V.iv

Final game of tied World Series

Doubt not of the day,
And that once gotten, doubt not of large pay.

—King Henry VI, Part III, IV, vii

First base coach to cocky baserunner

And thy mind stand to't, boy, steal away
bravely.

—All's Well That Ends Well, II.i

First–draft choice stuck in the minors

I am commanded here, and kept a coil with
"Too young," and "the next year," and "'tis too
early."

—All's Well That Ends Well, II.i

First–pitch swinger

How poor are they that have no patience.

—Othello, II.iii

First-round pick who never made it out of the minors

His promises were, as he then was, mighty;
But his performance, as he is now, nothing.
—King Henry VIII, IV.ii

First woman reporter to enter locker room

You have displaced the mirth, broke the good
    meeting
With most admired disorder.
—Macbeth, III.iv

Foul line call

Where is my judgment fled,
That censures falsely what they see aright?
If that be fair whereon my false eyes dote,
What means the world to say it is not so?
—Sonnet CXLVIII

4 for 4 with 6 RBI

A victory is twice itself when the achiever
    brings
home full numbers.
—Much Ado About Nothing, I.i

Franchise pitcher calls it quits

I will play no more to–night;
My mind's not on't; you are too hard for me.

—King Henry VIII, V.i

Free agent

Come, woo me, woo me; for now I am in
a holiday humour, and like enough to consent.

—As You Like It, IV.i

Frivolous bettor

A fool
That seest a game play'd home, the rich stake
    drawn,
And takest it all for jest.

—The Winter's Tale, I.ii

George Steinbrenner

Upon what meat doth this our Caesar feed,
That he is grown so great?

—Julius Caesar, I.ii

Giving up a walk to the 27th batter after 26 successive outs

I had else been perfect.

—Macbeth, III.iv

Glib but erratic infielder
They say, best men are moulded out of faults;
And, for the most, become much more the better
For being a little bad.
—Measure for Measure, V.i.

Glum manager
So, so, so, so:—they laugh that wins.
—Othello, IV.i

Goofy left fielder
I am too much i' the sun.
—Hamlet, I.ii

Graceful infielder
Custom hath made it in him a property of
easiness.
—Hamlet, V.i

Grammatically challenged but eager rookie
I will do
All my abilities in thy behalf.
—Othello, III.iii

Grand slam, theirs

O, horrible! O, horrible! most horrible!

—Hamlet, I.v

Grand slam, yours

O wonderful, wonderful and most wonderful
wonderful! and yet again wonderful, and after
    that,
out of all whooping!

—As You Like It, III.ii

Griping manager

Then give me leave; for losers will have leave
To ease their stomachs with their bitter tongues.

—Titus Andronicus, III.i

Grounds crew

Sweep on, you fat and greasy citizens!

—As You Like It, II.i

Groupies

Daughters of the game.

—Troilus and Cressida, IV.v

Grudge–bearing manager to umpire

I see no reason why thou shouldst be so
    superfluous
to demand the time of the day.

              –King Henry IV, Part I, I.ii

Hall of Fame candidate

I have
Immortal longings in me.

              –Antony and Cleopatra, V.ii

Hanging in there

Thou hast hit it; for there's no better sign of a
brave mind than a hard hand.

              –King Henry VI, Part II, IV.ii

Hank Aaron's 715th home run

Aaron, thou hast hit it.
              AARON
Would you had hit it too!
Then should not we be tired with this ado.

              –Titus Andronicus, II.i

Hard–luck manager

A fellow that hath had losses.
—Much Ado About Nothing, IV.ii

Hard–nosed umpire crew chief

"It will be rain to–night."
"Let it come down."
—Macbeth, III.iii

Haughty umpire to protesting manager

If you have any pity, grace, or manners,
You would not make me such an argument.
—A Midsummer Night's Dream, III.ii

Heckler who has moved to new league town

Whom should I knock?
—The Taming of the Shrew, I.ii

Hector Lopez waving off teammates

Hector shall have a great catch, and a knock
out either
of your brains.
—Troilus and Cressida, II.i

40

Hidaki Irabu on being sent to the bullpen

O me unhappy!

–The Two Gentlemen of Verona, V.iv

Hit batsman by visiting team, knockdown pitch by home team

Measure for Measure

Hit batsman charging the mound

By this hand, I will supplant some of your teeth.

–The Tempest, III.ii

Hitter who knows he's got a home run

True! pow, wow.

–Coriolanus, II.i

Hitting instructor

I understand the business, I hear it: to have an open ear,
a quick eye, and a nimble hand is necessary.

–The Winter's Tale, IV.iv

Home plate ump cutting short a mound conference

Break off the parley.

–King Henry VI, Part III, II.ii

Home run after arguing poor strike call on 3 and 0

Sweet are the uses of adversity.

–As You Like It, II.i

Honest but erratic fielder

Wrong hath but wrong, and blame the due of blame.

–King Richard III, V.i

"I got it! I got it!"

I'll catch it ere it come to ground.

–Macbeth, III.v

Indecision in Anaheim

I guess one Angel in another's hell.
Yet this shall I never know, but live in doubt,
Till my bad Angel fire my good one out.

–Sonnet CXLIV

Infield chatter

Thou canst not hit it, hit it, hit it,
Thou canst not hit it, my good man.

—Love's Labour's Lost, IV.i

Infield in with runners on first and third

I see the play so lies.

—The Winter's Tale, IV.iv

Injury prone

Like a strutting player, whose conceit
Lies in his hamstring, and doth think it rich
To hear the wooden dialogue and sound
'Twixt his stretched footage and the scaffoldage.

—Troilus and Cressida, I.iii

Inserting rookie into the lineup at last minute

Go, play, boy, play.

—The Winter's Tale, I.ii

Intentional walk

So thy great gift, upon misprision growing,
Comes home again . . .

—Sonnet LXXXVII

Interleague play
Much Ado About Nothing

Introducing Stan Musial
'Tis so.—
The Cardinal!

–King Henry VIII, III.ii

Invited to take part in charity game
Now name the rest of the players.

–A Midsummer Night's Dream, I.ll

Jimmy Carter on 1994 players' strike
Let me be umpire in this doubtful strife.

–King Henry VI, Part I, IV.i

Joe DiMaggio
Thou hast nor youth nor age;
But as it were, an after–dinner's sleep,
Dreaming on both.

–Measure for Measure, III.i

Joe Torre

Seldom he smiles, and smiles in such a sort
As if he mocked himself, and scorn'd his spirit
That could be moved to smile at anything.

—Julius Caesar, I.ii

Just outside the left–field pole

Foul is most foul.

—As You Like It, III.v

Just missed it

O! Ho! 'tis foul.

—King Lear, III.ii

Kindly manager to traded player

Men must endure
Their going hence, even as their coming hither.

—King Lear, V.ii

Kindly coach to picked–off runner

Come, come, come, come, give me your hand:
   what's
done cannot be undone.

—Macbeth, V.i

Knockdown pitch from former teammate

Who hateth thee that I do call my friend?
On whom frown'st thou that I do fawn upon?
Nay if thou low'rst on me, do I not spend
Revenge upon myself with present moan?

—Sonnet CXLIX

Last-place team looking for explanations

Or else 'twere hard luck, being in so preposterous
estate as we are.

—The Winter's Tale, V.ii

Late-night rebroadcast

Full of sound and fury,
Signifying nothing.

—Macbeth, V.v

Leadoff batter

'Twill do me good to walk.

—Othello, IV.iii

Leadoff walk, from fielding team's perspective

That is the true beginning of our end.

—A Midsummer Night's Dream, V.i

Leadoff walk, from batting team's perspective

Zounds!

—King John, II.i

League president, levying fines

With thy brawls thou hast disturb'd our sport.

—A Midsummer Night's Dream, II.I

Left–field wall in Fenway Park

It is the green–ey'd monster.

—Othello, III.iii

Losing streak

What potions have I drunk of Siren tears,
Distill'd from limbecs foul as hell within,
Applying fears to hopes, and hopes to fears,
Still losing when I saw myself to win!
What wretched errors hath my heart committed,
Whilst it hath thought itself so blessed never!

—Sonnet CXIX

Lost home–field advantage

Better at home, if "would I might" were
   "may."—
But to the sport abroad.

—Troilus and Cressida, I.i

Manager coming off a suspension

No, I will be the pattern of all patience; I will
say nothing.

—King Lear, III.ii

Manager filling out lineup card

Make you ready your stiff bats.

—Coriolanus, I.i

Manager firing

If it were done when 'tis done, then 'twere well
It were done quickly.

—Macbeth, I.vi

Manager reviewing lineup

There I have another bad match.

—The Merchant of Venice, III.i

MUCH ADO ABOUT NOTHING

Manager with a bench loaded with talent

I will use them according to their desert.

–Hamlet, II.ii

Manager's tough fifth–inning decision

The sun doth burn my face; I must remove.

–Venus and Adonis, l. 186

Mark McGwire

O, that record is lively in my soul!

–Twelfth Night, V.i

Mike Schmidt's farewell news conference

The big round tears
Cours'd one another down his innocent nose,
In piteous chase.

–As You Like It, II.i

Missed sign

Then my dial goes not true: I took this lark for a bunting.

–All's Well That Ends Well, II.v

Mound conference

O! there has been much throwing about of brains.

—Hamlet, II.ii

Mound meeting in Arlington, Texas, in July

Fie! This is hot weather, gentlemen.

—King Henry IV, Part II, III.ii

Moving billboards

We are advertis'd by our loving friends.

—King Henry VI, Part III, V.iii

National League fan's opinion of the other league

Shameful is this league!

—King Henry VI, Part II, I.i

Natural Athlete

If thou dost play with him at any game,
Thou art sure to lose.

—Antony and Cleopatra, II.iii

51

New bat
Why, this hits right.

—Timon of Athens, III.i

New Central American player
I cannot tell what the dickens his name is.

—The Merry Wives of Windsor, III.ii

New pitch developed off–season
An ill–favored thing, sir, but mine own.

—As You Like It, V.iv

New sun shades
What a pair of spectacles is here!

—Troilus and Cressida, IV.iv

New TV contract
This sport, well carried, shall be chronicled.

—A Midsummer Night's Dream, III.ii

New York Mets and/or Chicago Cubs
Past hope, past cure, past help!

—Romeo and Juliet, IV.i

Nice–guy pitcher

Give me thy hand: I'm sorry that I beat thee.
—*The Tempest, III.ii*

Nolan Ryan

We that are young
Shall never see so much, nor live so long.
—*King Lear, V.iii*

Number one draft pick

Why, then the world's mine oyster.
—*The Merry Wives of Windsor, II.ii*

0 for 4, struck out three times

We have seen better days.
—*Timon of Athens, IV.ii*

Official scorekeeper

If this be error, and upon me prov'd,
I never writ.
—*Sonnet CXVI*

Old-fashioned outfielder
I should be still
Plucking the grass, to know where sits the wind.
—The Merchant of Venice, I.i

Old players versus modern
Then what they do in present,
Though less than yours in past, must o'ertop
yours.
—Troilus and Cressida, III.iii

Old timers' day
If pleased themselves, others, they think,
delight
In such like circumstance, with such like sport:
Their copious stories, oftentimes begun,
End without audience, and are never done.
—Venus and Adonis, ll. 844–47

Out-of-town scoreboard
Who loses and who wins; who's in, who's out.
—King Lear, V.iii

Outfielder losing ball in the sun

Give me some help here. Ho!
> —*All's Well That Ends Well, II.i*

Overweight superstar on spring training

My salad days.
> —*Antony and Cleopatra, I.v*

Owner to his championship team

Go together,
You precious winners all; your exultation
Partake to every one.
> —*The Winter's Tale, V.iii*

Owner to his championship team who have filed for free agency

How sharper than a serpent's tooth it is.
> —*King Lear, I.iv*

Owners' meeting

The first thing we do, let's kill all the lawyers.
> —*King Henry VI, Part II, IV.ii*

IF I GO TO HIM, WITH MY ARMED FIST
I'LL PASH HIM OE'R THE FACE

TROILUS AND CRESSIDA II iii

PITCHER AWAITING CHARGING BATSMAN

Pete Rose leaves the game

So farewell to the little good you bear me.
Farewell, a long farewell, to all my greatness!
This is the state of man: to–day he puts forth
The tender leaves of hope; to–morrow blossoms,
And bears his blushing honours thick upon him;
The third day comes a frost, a killing frost,
And—when he thinks, good easy man, full
   surely
His greatness is a–ripening—nips his root,
And then he falls, as I do.
                  –King Henry VIII, III.ii

Perfect game

A Midsummer Night's Dream

Pesky baserunner

Either master the devil or throw him out.
                  –Hamlet, III.iv

Philosophical Boston fan

Ay, that way goes the game.
         –A Midsummer Night's Dream, III.ii

Pinch hitters

They basely fly, and dare not stay the field.

—Venus and Adonis, l. 894

Pinch runner – I

Now bid me run,
And I will strive with things impossible.

—Julius Caesar, II.i

Pinch runner – II

Thou thy worldly task hast done,
Home art gone and ta'en thy wages.

—Cymbeline, IV.ii

Pitcher acquired as low end of a trade

Such unconstant starts are we like to have
from him.

—King Lear, I.i

Pitcher after receiving pep talk from coach

Why, so! then am I sure of victory.
Now therefore let us hence.

—King Henry VI, Part III, IV.i

58

Pitcher covering first

I see the play so lies
That I must bear a part.

—The Winter's Tale, IV.iv

Pitcher joining team after salary hold-out

And when I start, the envious people laugh,
And bid me be advised how I tread.

—Henry VI, Part II, II, iv

Pitcher just brought up from the minors

This is the night
That either makes me or foredoes me quite.

—Othello, V.i

Pitcher returning to dugout after being removed

Throw thy glove,
Or any token of thy honour else.

—Timon of Athens, V.iv

Pitcher with a moving fast ball

I have a kind of alacrity in sinking.
—The Merry Wives of Windsor, III.v

Pitcher with poor playoff record

Was there ever any man thus beaten out of
    season,
When in the why and the wherefore is neither rime
    nor reason?
—The Comedy of Errors, II.ii

Pitcher who starts thinking
instead of throwing

And thus the native hue of resolution
Is sicklied o'er with the pale cast of thought.
—Hamlet, III.i

Pitcher's game plan

To mow 'em down before me.
—King Henry VIII, V.iii

Player new to New York

Methinks I should not thus be led along,
Mail'd up in shame, with papers on my back,

And follow'd with a rabble, that rejoice
To see my tears and hear my deep–fet groans.
–Henry VI, Part II, II, iv

Player with bonus clause in contract

Why, nothing comes amiss, so money comes
withal.
–The Taming of the Shrew, I.ii

Player's agent

I could never better stead thee than now.
Put money
in thy purse. . . . Fill thy purse with
money. . . . Make
all the money thou canst. . . . Therefore make
money.
. . . Go, make money. . . . Provide thy money.
Go to,
farewell! put money enough in your purse.
–Othello, I.iii

Playing tough

Do with your injuries as seems you best.
–Measure for Measure, V.i

BUT NOW I AM CABIN'D, CRIBB'D CONFINED, BOUND IN
TO SAUCY DOUBTS AND FEARS

MACBETH, III, IV

PUT ON THE DL

Poor April starter

For this relief much thanks; 'tis bitter cold
And I am sick at heart.

—Hamlet, I.i

Poor attendance figures

A beggarly account of empty boxes.

—Romeo and Juliet, V.i

Poor fielding pitcher

I will fear to catch it, and give way; when I know
not what else to do.

—Timon of Athens, IV.iii

Poor–hitting team decides to play "little ball"

If our betters play at that game, we must not dare
To imitate them.

—Timon of Athens, I.ii

Poor infielder

In faith I do not love thee with mine eyes,
For they in thee a thousand errors note.

—Sonnet CXLI

BE SURE OF IT; GIVE ME THE OCULAR PROOF.

OTHELLO, III iii

QUESTIONABLE STRIKE CALL

Poor loser
The game was ne'er so fair, and I am done.
—Romeo and Juliet, I.iv

Poor losers sitting out off-season
Now is the winter of our discontent.
—King Richard III, I.i

Poor personal habits
When they are out, they will spit.
—As You Like It, IV.i

Poor pickoff move
This was look'd for at your hand, and this was balk'd.
—Twelfth Night, III.ii

Poor relief pitcher
Having nothing, nothing can he lose.
—King Henry VI, Part III, III.iii

Poor line umpire
Fair is foul, and foul is fair.
—Macbeth, I.i

Poorly executed hit–and–run

Like a dull actor now,
I have forgot my part, and I am out.

–Coriolanus, V.iii

Potential switch hitter

To be or not to be; that is the question.

–Hamlet, III.i

Preparation crew

Flout 'em and scout 'em;
And scout 'em and flout 'em.

–The Tempest, III.ii

Probable new owner of losing club

A merchant of incomparable wealth.

–The Taming of the Shrew, IV.ii

Protesting manager approaches umpire

Here will be an old abusing of God's patience
and the king's English.

–The Merry Wives of Windsor, I.iv

Prying sportswriter

The players cannot keep counsel; they'll tell all.

–Hamlet, III.ii

Questionable trade

Let me not to the marriage of true minds
Admit impediments.

–Sonnet CXVI

Rally

Come.—Another hit; what say you?

–Hamlet, V.ii

Reaction to newspaper editorial on decline of the game

Then with the losers let it sympathise,
For nothing can seem foul to those that win.

–King Henry IV, Part I, V.i

Randy Johnson

What an arm he has!

–Coriolanus, IV.v

Reggie Jackson in unaccustomed guise

Not stepping o'er the bounds of modesty.

—Romeo and Juliet, IV.ii

Reinstated suspended player

So you walk softly, and look sweetly, and say
nothing.

—Much Ado About Nothing, II.i

Reliever after walking three and giving up a hit

I am gone.

—Cymbeline, I.i

Repect for the game

One business does command us all; for mine
Is money.

—Timon of Athens, III.iv

Reply to visiting team that predicts a sweep

You forget
That we are those which chased you from the
field.

—King Henry VI, Part III, I.i

Retaliation pitch
If I can catch him once upon the hip,
I will feed fat the ancient grudge I bear him.
—The Merchant of Venice, I.iii

Retired umpire
I know myself now; and I feel within me
A peace within all earthly dignities,
A still and quiet conscience.
—King Henry VIII, III.ii

Retirement
When to the sessions of sweet silent thought
I summon up remembrance of things past.
—Sonnet XXX

Return to the dugout after striking out
When from high—most pitch, with weary car,
Like feeble age, he reeleth from the day,
The eyes, 'fore duteous, now converted are
From his low tract, and look another way.
—Sonnet VII

Rickey Henderson
What a piece of work.
—Hamlet, II.ii

Road secretary

Good my lord, will you see the players well
    bestowed?
Do you hear, let them be well used.

–Hamlet, II

Road trip hijinks

And therefore, living hence, did give ourself
To barbarous licence; as 'tis ever common
That men are merriest when they are from home.

–King Henry V, I.ii

Robert Merrill

For my voice, —I have lost it with hallooing,
    and singing
of anthems.

–King Henry IV, Part II, I.ii

Roberto Alomar on a certain umpire

I do defy him, and I spit on him.

–King Richard II, I.i

Rookie brushing off batting coach

I have a good eye, uncle.
—*Much Ado About Nothing, II.i*

Rookie looking for his first double

I yet am unprovided
Of a pair of bases.
—*Pericles, II.i*

Rumored trade

There is something in the wind.
—*The Comedy of Errors, III.i*

Runners on first and second, two outs

Primo, secundo, tertio, is a good play.
—*Twelfth Night, V.i*

Rupert Murdoch's purchase of the Dodgers

If there be more, more woeful, hold it in;
For I am almost ready to dissolve,
Hearing of this.
—*King Lear, V.iii*

72

Salutes to fans from Ted Williams, Jack McDowell, Albert Belle, et al.

Je pense qu'ils sont appelés de fingres; *oui,* de fingres.

−King Henry V, III.iv

Sammy Sosa

I thank my god for my humility.

−King Richard III, II.i

Sarcastic platooned player studying lineup

'Tis a playing day, I see.

−The Merry Wives of Windso, IV.i

Sarcastic second backup catcher to manager

I humbly thank your highness;
And am right glad to catch this good occasion.

−King Henry VIII, V.i

Satisfied fans

And, being a winner, God give you good night.

−The Taming of the Shrew, V.ii

Savvy outfielder

He knows the game: how true he keeps the
  wind!

–King Henry VI, Part III, III.ii

Scattered hits

They did battery to the spheres intend;
Sometimes diverted their poor balls are ty'd
To the orb'd earth; sometimes they do extend
To view right on.

–A Lover's Complaint

Scott Boras

O world! world! world! thus is the poor agent
despised.

–Troilus and Cressida, V.x

Scouts' reports

The bookish theoric.

–Othello, I.i

Season's opener

The uncertain glory of an April day,
Which now shows all the beauty of the sun,
And by and by a cloud takes all away!

–The Two Gentlemen of Verona, I.iii

Season's ups and downs

The end crowns all;
And that old common arbitrator, Time,
Will one day end it.

—Troilus and Cressida, IV.v

Second-place club going against league leader

The harder match'd, the greater victory.

—King Henry VI, Part III, V.i

Secret to success

The play's the thing.

—Hamlet, II.ii

Security guard directed to unruly fan

I'll see what I can do.

—Measure for Measure, I.iv

Self-justifying manager

Who can be wise, amazed, temperate and
    furious,
Loyal and neutral, in a moment? No man.

—Macbeth, II.iii

Shortening lead after nearly being picked off base

But hold thee still;
Things bad begun make strong themselves by ill.
—*Macbeth, III.ii*

Showboat

Is it not monstrous that this player here,
But in a fiction, in a dream of passion,
Could force his soul so to his own conceit.
—*Hamlet, II.ii*

Showing bunt

So slides he down upon his grained bat.
—*A Lover's Complaint, l. 64*

Sidearm delivery

Why, 'tis a boisterous and a cruel style,
A style for challengers.
—*As You Like It, IV.iii*

Slugging team disdains "little ball"

We detest such vile base practices.
—*The Two Gentlemen of Verona, IV.i*

Slump breaker

A hit, a very palpable hit.

—Hamlet, V.ii

Slumping hitter with drug problem

A little pot and soon hot.

—The Taming of the Shrew, IV.i

Small sympathy from team trainer

There be some sports are painful.

—The Tempest, III.i

Soft hands

No doubt but he hath got a quiet catch.

—The Taming of the Shrew, II.i

Sports announcer

That tongue that tells the story of thy days,
Making lascivious comments on thy sport,
Cannot dispraise but in a kind of praise;
Naming thy name blesses an ill report.

—Sonnet XCV

Spring training, first day

How many goodly creatures are there here!
How beauteous mankind is! O brave new world,
That has such people in't.

—The Tempest, V.i

Spring training, last day

This was the most unkindest cut of all.

—Julius Caesar, III.ii

Squeeze play in one–sided game

What need'st thou wound with cunning, when
    thy might
Is more than my o'erpress'd defence can 'bide?

—Sonnet CXXXIX

Stands vendors

Come buy of me, come; come buy, come buy;
Buy lads.

—The Winter's Tale, IV.iii

Stats, favorable

Thy gift, thy tables, are within my brain
Full character'd with lasting memory,

Which shall above that idle rank remain,
Beyond all date, even to eternity;
Or at the least so long as brain and heart
Have faculty by nature to subsist;
Till each to raz'd oblivion yield his part
Of thee, thy record never can be miss'd.
                                        –Sonnet CXXII

Stats, unfavorable

Thy registers and thee I both defy,
Not wondering at the present nor the past;
For thy records and what we see do lie.
                                        –Sonnet CXXIII

Stealing second on a fast–ball pitcher

Run, run! O run!
                                        –King Lear, V.iii

Stealing second in a hopeless game

There's honour in the theft.
                                –All's Well That Ends Well, II.i

Stealing third with two out

O! that way madness lies; let me shun that.
                                        –King Lear, III.iv

Struck out by Rich Gossage

The devil damn thee black, thou cream–faced
loon!
Where gott'st thou that goose look?
–Macbeth, V.iii

Struck out looking

There let him stand, and rave.
–Titus Andronicus, V.iii

Struck out swinging

The destinies will curse thee for this stroke.
–Venus and Adonis, l. 946

Struck out with bases loaded

And after that, he came, thus sad, away.
–Julius Caesar, I.ii

Successful beginning to midwest road trip

Thus far into the bowels of the land
Have we marched on without impediment.
–King Richard III, V.ii

Suicide squeeze

Go home,
And show no sign of fear.

—Coriolanus, IV.vi

Superstar with only one homer at end of May

'Tis but early days.

—Troilus and Cressida, IV.v

Superstar with weight clause in contract

O! that this too too sullied flesh would melt,
Thaw and resolve itself into a dew.

—Hamlet, I.ii

Superstar's temper tantrums

The lives of all your living complices
Lean on your health; the which if you give o'er
To stormy passion, must perforce decay.

—King Henry IV, Part II, I.i

Suspected corked bat

There is something in this more than natural, if
philosophy could find it out.

—Hamlet, II.ii

IF I CANNOT WARD WHAT I WOULD NOT HAVE HIT
I CAN WATCH YOU FOR TELLING HOW I TOOK THE BLOW;
UNLESS IT SWELL PAST HIDING.

TROILUS AND CRESSIDA. I ii

TAKING ONE FOR THE TEAM

Swinging for the fences

Imagination of some great exploit
Drives him beyond the bounds of patience.

—King Henry IV, Part I, I.iii

Tactless interviewer to losing pitcher

You were lately whipt, sir, as I think.

—All's Well That Ends Well, II.ii

Take–out slide

Tell me, you heavens, in which part of his body
Shall I destroy him?

—Troilus and Cressida, IV.v

Taken out in the sixth with comfortable lead

His cares are now all ended.

—King Henry IV, Part II, V.ii

Talking a good game

For it comes to pass oft, that a terrible oath, with
a swaggering accent sharply twang'd off, gives
manhood more approbation than ever proof
   itself
would have earn'd him.

—Twelfth Night, III.iv

Team player

Pray you, let's hit together.

–King Lear, I.i

Teammates

To say they err, I dare not be so bold,
Although I swear it to myself alone.
And, to be sure that is not false I swear,
A thousand groans.

–Sonnet CXXXI

Ted Turner's new stadium

The diamond,—why, 'twas beautiful and hard,
Whereto his invised properties did tend;
The deep–green emerald, in whose fresh regard
Weak sights their sickly radiance do amend.

–A Lover's Complaint, ll. 211–14

Ted Williams's last at bat

You have hit it.

–King Henry IV, Part I, II.iv

Tenth man up in same inning

The wheel is come full circle; I am here.

–King Lear, V.iii

This year's signer of all–time record contract

What piles of wealth he hath accumulated
To his own portion!

—King Henry VIII, III.ii

Thoughts while leading off second

I would I were at home.

—As You Like It, IV.iii

Threat of rain in third inning while behind 10 and 0

Such sweet thunder.

—A Midsummer Night's Dream, IV.i

Third–base coach

Will he give you the nod?

—Troilus and Cressida, I.ii

Third–base coach to indifferent baserunner

Be wise, and get you home.

—Othello, V.ii

CONFUSION NOW HATH MADE HIS MASTERPIECE

MACBETH. II ii

Third baseman playing close to the bag

As fearfully as doth a galled rock
O'erhang and jutty his confounded base.
–King Henry V, III.i

Thrown out trying to stretch a double into a triple

God save the mark!
–King Henry IV, Part I, I.iii

Time for retirement – I

Is it not strange that desire should so many
    years
outlive performance.
–King Henry IV, Part II, II.iv

Time for Retirement – II

I have not that alacrity of spirit,
Nor cheer of mind that I was wont to have.
–King Richard III, V.iii

Timid baserunner holding up at third

You come not home, because you have
no stomach.
                        −The Comedy of Errors, I.ii

Tossed from game

Nay, let me alone for swearing.
                        −Twelfth Night, III.iv

Tossed from hopeless game

Kind umpire of men's miseries,
With sweet enlargement doth dimiss me hence.
                        −King Henry VI, Part I, II.v

Tough left field

So bedazzled with the sun
That everything I look on seemeth green.
                        −The Taming of the Shrew, IV.v

Traded player

In nothing am I chang'd
But in my garments
                        −King Lear, IV.iv

Trailing with two down in the bottom of the ninth

There's hope in't yet.

—Antony and Cleopatra, III.xiii

Troublesome hitter

Would he were knockt i'th' head.

—Troilus and Cressida, IV.ii

TV replay shows that strike was clearly a ball

He hath cause to complain.

—Measure for Measure, II.i

20–game loser

How weary, stale, flat, and unprofitable
Seem to me all the uses of this world!

—Hamlet, I.ii

20–game winner

He capers, he dances, he has eyes of youth, he
writes verses, he speaks holiday, he smells
    April
and May: he will carry't; 'tis in his buttons; he
will carry't.

—The Merry Wives of Windsor, III.ii

.200 HITTER

THOU HAST NO EYES TO SEE,
BUT HATEFULLY AT RANDOM DOST THOU HIT

VENUS AND ADONIS, ll. 939-40

Two–base hit after working count to 3 and 2

Double, double, toil and trouble.

—Macbeth, IV.i

Two expansion teams meet in interleague play

The Comedy of Errors

Two runners ending up on second

Confusion now hath made his masterpiece!

—Macbeth, II.ii

Ty Cobb

I grow, I prosper;
Now, gods, stand up for bastards!

—King Lear, I.ii

Umpire crew chief to protesting managers

Seal up the mouth of outrage for awhile,
Till we can clear these ambiguities.

—Romeo and Juliet, V.iii

Umpires

Is there any cause in nature that makes these
hard hearts?

–King Lear, III.vi

Umpires' new uniforms

O, 'tis the cunning livery of hell.

–Measure for Measure, III.i

Umpire's privilege

It is in my power
To o'erthrow law, and in one self–born hour
To plant and o'erwhelm custom.

–The Winter's Tale, V.Chorus IV.i

Umpire to raging manager

I beseech you, sir,
Harm not yourself with your vexation;
I am senseless of your wrath.

–Cymbeline, I.i

Umpire to Roberto Alomar

Here. Why dost thou spit at me?

–King Richard III, I.ii

Unconventional stance

By God's sonties, 'twill be a hard way to hit.

—The Merchant of Venice, II.ii

Union negotiations

Idle words, servants to shallow fools!
Unprofitable sounds, weak arbitrators!
Busy yourself in skill–contending schools;
Debate where leisure serves with dull debaters;
To trembling clients be you mediators.

—Rape of Lucrece, l. 1017–21

Unlikely happening

And set the triple crown upon his head.

—King Henry VI, Part II, I.iii

Upon learning that Randy Johnson has been traded to your rival

I have heard better news.

—King Henry IV, Part II, II.i

Upstart rookie

Is there no respect of place, persons, nor time, in you?

—Twelfth Night, II.iii

Uptight manager to his too loose players

God hath given you one face, and you make
yourselves
another: you jig, you amble, and you lisp, and
nickname
God's creatures, and make your wantonness your
ignorance. Go to, I'll no more on't; it hath
made me mad.

—Hamlet, III.i

Utility infielder

I do perceive here a divided duty.

—Othello, I.iii

Veteran challenged for his position

I am as able and fit as thou.

—Titus Andronicus, II.i

Veteran hitter

Look you what hacks are on his helmet! look you
yonder, do you see? look you there: there's no
jesting;
there's no laying on, tak't off who will, as they say:
there be hacks!

—Troilus and Cressida, I.ii

Veteran picked up by owner of expansion team

I will win for him an I can; if not, I will gain
    nothing but
my own shame and the odd hits.

—Hamlet, V.ii

Visiting teams' locker rooms

These dreary dumps.

—Titus Andronicus, I.i

Vociferous fans

How earnestly they knock!

—Troilus and Cressida, IV.ii

Wait till next year

Make glad and sorry seasons, as thou fleetest,
And do whate'er thou wilt, swift–footed Time.

—Sonnet XIX

Waved around third

As manhood shall compound: push home.

—King Henry V, II.i

West coast team about to come up against the Yankees

Thus far our fortune keeps an upward course,
And we are graced with wreaths of victory.
But, in the midst of this bright–shining day,
I spy a black, suspicious, threatening cloud,
That will encounter with our glorious sun
Ere he attain his easeful western bed.
—King Henry VI, Part III, V.iii

Whining pitcher coming off an 8–run first inning

I ne'er had worse luck in my life.
—All's Well That Ends Well, II.ii

Whirlpool treatment

Diseases desperate grown
By desperate appliances are relieved,
Or not at all.
—Hamlet, IV.iii

Wide strike zone, from batters' perspective

O vile,
Intolerable, not to be endured!
—The Taming of the Shrew, V.ii

Wide strike zone, from pitchers' perspective

A thousand times more fair, ten thousand times more rich.

—The Merchant of Venice, III.ii

Wild swing

Ho! now you strike like the blind man.

—Much Ado About Nothing, II.i

Wind sprints

Jog on, jog on, the footpath way.

—The Winter's Tale, IV.iii

Willie Mays's catch in the 1954 World Series

Before my God, I might not this believe
Without the sensible and true avouch
Of mine own eyes.

—Hamlet, I.i

World Series loss

For God's sake, let us sit upon the ground
And tell sad stories of the death of kings.

—King Richard II, III.ii

World Series win

It shall be raging mad, and silly mild,
Make the young old, the old become a child.
—Venus and Adonis, ll. 1151–52

Yankee Stadium's future

Cry woe, destruction, ruin, loss, decay.
—King Richard II, III.ii

Yogi Berra on the art of catching

None are so surely caught, when they are catcht.
—Love's Labour's Lost, V.ii

Yogi Berra on the vicissitudes of the game

All's Well That Ends Well

"You could look it up"

It is upon record, or else reported
Successively from age to age?
—King Richard III, III.i

Post-Game Show

Shakespeare's curses and insults are one of the glories of our culture and we would be remiss if we did not include them in a collection of his baseball writings. Unfortunately, they cannot be tied to any specific game situation or personality. Therefore, we have arranged a few in a contrived scene. So, imagine if you will . . .

A Baseball Stadium

Enter MANAGER *and* UMPIRE. FANS, REPORTERS, *and* PHOTOGRAPHERS *above*.

MANAGER

Good dawning to thee, friend. Fellow, I know thee for a knave; a rascal; an eater of broken meats; a base, proud, shallow, beggarly, three–suited, hundred–pound, filthy, worsted–stocking knave; a lily–liver'd, action–taking, whoreson, glass–gazing, superserviceable, finical rogue; one–trunk–inheriting slave; one that wouldst be a bawd in way of good service, and art nothing but the composition of a knave, begger, coward, pandar, and the son and heir of a mongrel bitch; one whom I will beat into clamorous whining. if thou deniest the least syllable of thy addition: an adulterous thief, an hypocrite, a virgin–violator!

FANS

Oh!

UMPIRE

And a good morrow to thee, sir, thou sod-
den–witted lord! thou hast no more brain than I
have in my elbows; an assinego may tutor thee:
thou scurvy–valiant ass! thou art here but to
thrash; and thou art bought and sold among those
of any wit, like a barbarian slave, thou thing of no
bowels, thou! who wears his wits in his belly and
his guts in his head. I wouldst thou the rotten diseases of the south, the guts–griping, ruptures,
catarrhs, loads o'gravel i'th'back, lethargies, cold
palsies, raw eyes, dirt–rotten livers, wheezing
lungs, bladders full of imposthume, sciaticas,
limekilns i'th'palm, incurable bone–ache, and the
rivell'd fee–simple of the tetter, take and take
again such discoveries!

MANAGER

You ruinous butt; you whoreson indistin-
guishable cur; thou idle immaterial skein of
sleeve–silk, thou green sarcernet flap for a sore
eye, thou tassel of a prodigal's purse, thou! Ah,
how the poor world is pester'd with such water-
flies,—diminutives of nature! [*Aside*] I would
tread this unbolted villain into mortar, and daub
the walls of a jakes with him.

UMPIRE

Thou whoreson zed! thou unnecessary letter!
Get thee hence! Gone! Out!

MANAGER

Fie on't!

[Exit, pursued by REPORTERS.]